Common Duiker in the Northern Savanna

Books in the Wildlife of the World series:

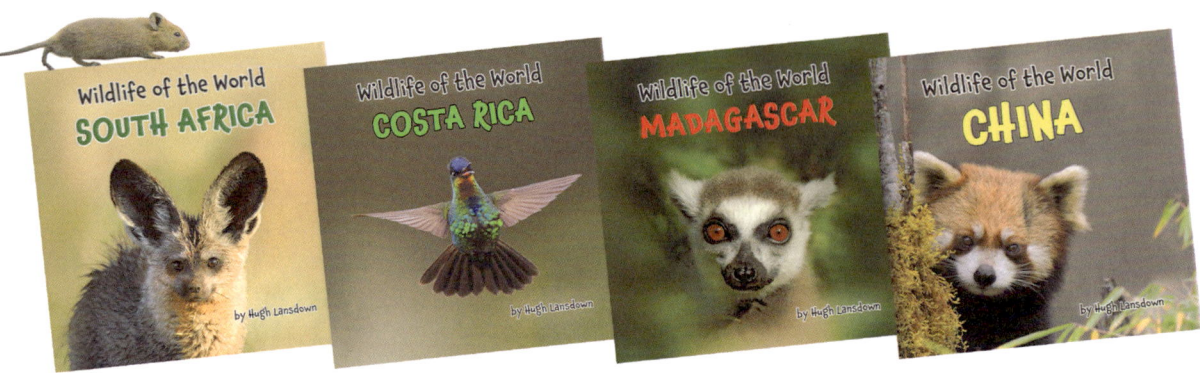

Wildlife of the World - South Africa
Wildlife of the World - Costa Rica
Wildlife of the World - Madagascar
Wildlife of the World - China

Coming soon:
Wildlife of the World - Japan

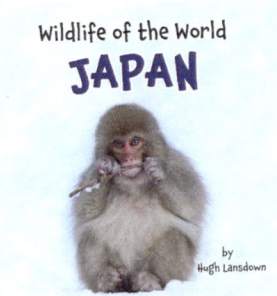

Visit *www.wildlifeoftheworld.com* to find out more about the books in the Wildlife of the World series.

Wildlife of the World
South Africa

by

Hugh Lansdown

Text copyright © Hugh Lansdown 2024
Photography copyright © Hugh Lansdown 2024
All rights reserved.
ISBN: 978-1-917175-04-3

Hugh Lansdown has asserted his right under the Copyright, Designs and Patent Act 1988 to be identified as the author of this work.

This book is meant to be educational, informative and entertaining. Although the author and publisher have made every effort to ensure that the information in this book was correct at the time of publication, the author and publisher do not assume and hereby disclaim any liability to any party for loss, damage or disruption caused by errors or omissions, whether such errors or omissions result from negligence, accident or any other cause.

The names given to animals in the book and associated online media are the most appropriate English names the author was able to find based on visible characteristics. They don't represent a precise scientific identification, which in many cases would require the animal to be captured and a detailed examination carried out.

First published 2024
by Natural Planet Books
Unit 134893
PO Box 7169
Poole
BH15 9EL

www.naturalplanetbooks.com

Library Cataloguing in Publication Data. A catalogue record for this book is available from the British Library.

All rights reserved. No part of this book may be reprinted or reproduced or utilised in any form or by electronic, mechanical or any other means, now known or hereafter invented, including photocopying or recording, or in any information storage or retrieval system, without the permission in writing from the publisher.

To Olivia

How to use this book

This is an 'Interactive' book, which means that as well as paper pages, it has digital ones containing videos, sound and slideshows.

How do I access the digital pages?

1. By scanning the QR codes

Throughout the book you will see Interactive Zones which look like this:

Just scan the black and white QR codes using a mobile phone, tablet or any device with a camera that can read QR codes.

2. By searching the Internet

If your device doesn't have a camera or can't read QR codes, you can just search the Internet for:

- **Hugh Lansdown photography**
- then click on **Books**
- **Wildlife of the World - South Africa**
- **Media Links**

You'll see a list of all the digital pages with the page number in this book that each one is linked to.

Wildlife Extras!

Some wildlife pages in this book have hidden animals that haven't been labelled. See how many you can spot then check the list on page 50 to see if you got them all!

Contents

	Page
How to use this book	6
Map of South Africa	8
Where is South Africa?	9
Ecological Regions	10
Savanna	11
Thickets and Woodland	15
Highveld Grasslands	19
Fynbos	23
Karoo	27
The Coast	31
Iconic South African Animals	35
African Penguins	36
Herbivores	38
Chacma Baboons	40
Carnivores	42
Meerkats	44
Conserving South Africa's Wildlife	46
Wildlife Extras	50

Where is South Africa?

South Africa is a large country on the southern tip of the African continent, between warm, tropical central Africa and the cold southern oceans.

This special location makes it a biodiversity hotspot, which means there are lots and lots of different types of animals and many live nowhere else in the world.

It's the most technically advanced African country, although there are still problems with poverty. It is known as the 'Rainbow Nation' because of the many different cultures, languages and religions.

Well duh!... It's in southern Africa!

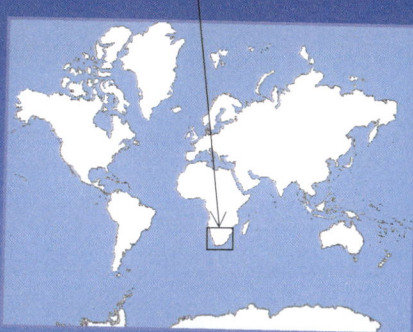

Ecological Regions

As you'd expect from one of the world's major biodiversity hotspots, South Africa has lots of different regions, each with its own special habitat and wildlife. These are the ones featured in this book:

- **Savanna**
- **Thickets and Woodland**
- **Highveld Grasslands**
- **Fynbos**
- **Karoo**
- **The Coast**

Try loading the **Interactive Map** and clicking the buttons to see the location of the different ecological regions. You can also see some major towns and cities as well as the national parks and reserves where many photos in this book were taken.

INTERACTIVE ZONE!

Scan the QR code to explore the interactive map

(If you're not sure how, check page 6 for details.)

Martial Eagle

Savanna

In the past, much of eastern Africa was covered in warm, dry grassland with scattered trees, called savanna. Home to huge herds of herbivores and the carnivores that hunt them, savanna is still found in parts of South Africa.

The **cheetah** is the fastest land animal, while the **martial eagle** is one of the world's most powerful birds… and both are specialist savanna predators.

Cheetah

WHAT LIVES IN THE SAVANNA?

The trees that grow in savanna are very important for the wildlife that lives there. They provide shade from the hot sun and a place to build a nest or hide from predators.

Strange-looking **yellow-billed hornbills** nest in holes in savanna trees. Once the female has laid her eggs, the male traps her inside by blocking the entrance with dried mud, just leaving a narrow slit so he can pass food in to her and the chicks. When the chicks are fully grown, the female smashes the dried mud with her huge beak to break them out of their nest prison!

Huge **kori bustards** are the biggest flying birds in Africa, though they prefer to stay on the ground and run away from danger on their powerful legs. They are important in some African cultures, often seen in rock paintings and featured in traditional dances.

Yellow-billed Hornbill

Kori Bustard

HOW DO THEY SURVIVE THERE?

Giraffes are the world's tallest animal, with extremely long necks to reach the tops of savanna trees. They have a super-powerful heart to pump blood all the way up to their head, and a long, flexible tongue that can grab hold of leaves and pluck them off the trees!

The pretty **African common white** is a savanna butterfly that will fly hundreds of kilometres to find a suitable place to lay its eggs. Sometimes, thousands gather and travel together in huge swarms.

Mother and Baby Giraffe

African Common White

INTERACTIVE ZONE!

Scan the QR code to see more elephant relatives

(If you're not sure how, check page 6 for details.)

Elephants and Their Strange Relatives!

The strange **aardvark** below looks a bit like a mix between a rabbit, a donkey and a pig, but it's actually a member of the Afrotheria family, which includes elephants and sea cows!

Visit the Interactive Zone to watch some more Afrotheria, or try the **Interactive Map** on page 10 to see where South African savanna is located.

Aardvark

Thickets and Woodland

South Africa's warm, dry climate means there isn't a lot of forest, but to the south and east, thickets of thorny bushes and dense woodland provide shelter for some special animals.

African elephants feed on the bushes and are the world's largest land animals, weighing up to 10 tons! **Red-faced mousebirds** scramble about in the thickets in small, noisy groups, searching for fruit and seeds to eat.

Red-faced Mousebird

African Elephants

WHAT LIVES IN THE THICKETS...

Thickets and woodland make excellent cover for animals threatened by hunting or poaching, and also provide a safe place for birds to build their nests.

Male **double-collared sunbirds** are beautifully coloured little birds that sing loudly from the tops of trees and bushes. Meanwhile, the brown, camouflaged female is working hard to build their nest, deep in a thicket.

South Africa has more types of tortoise than any other country. The biggest is the **leopard tortoise**, which can weigh up to 40 kilograms and live to be 100 years old! They are found throughout the country but prefer thorny thickets where they can hide from the people who collect them illegally for food or the pet trade.

Male Double-collared Sunbird

Leopard Tortoise

The **African buffalo** is a large member of the cow family that likes to shelter in South Africa's thickets and woodland. They live in large family groups and are very aggressive... occasionally they've even been known to kill lions that tried to attack them! Unfortunately, numbers in South Africa are falling due to habitat loss and poaching.

Rhinos are also endangered by poaching for their horns, which are popular in Chinese medicine. There are two types of rhino in South Africa. White rhinos feed on grass and live mainly in the savanna, while **black rhinos** feed on the leaves of shrubs and bushes in dense thickets.

...AND IN THE WOODLAND?

African Buffalo

Black Rhinoceros

INTERACTIVE ZONE!

Scan the QR code to watch elephants and dung beetles

(If you're not sure how, check page 6 for details.)

Elephant Clean-up Crew!

Big animals produce big poo, so imagine how much a herd of elephants leaves behind. Luckily, South African thickets have a special team to clear it up... by eating it! Female **giant dung beetles** lay their eggs in the poo, and the young grubs live inside, feeding on it.

Visit the Interactive Zone to watch some giant dung beetles, or try the **Interactive Map** on page 10 to see where woods and thickets are located.

Giant Flightless Dung Beetle

Highveld Grasslands

Highveld is the name given to a large area of plateau in central South Africa that used to be covered in grass. Most has been replaced by crops and industry now, but there are still some areas where special grassland animals live.

The noisy **Cape grassbird** searches for small insects in the tall grass, where it also builds it's little nest. Agile **four-striped grass mice** forage for seeds down below, keeping a sharp eye out for predators like the yellow mongoose.

Cape Grassbird

Four-striped Grass Mouse

WHAT LIVES IN THE GRASSLANDS?

Although the central plateau is the most industrialised and developed part of South Africa, there's still lots of wildlife in special protected areas.

Endangered **blue cranes** are South Africa's national bird. They breed mainly in the Highveld, where couples perform a complicated courtship dance before raising one or two chicks. They fight fiercely to protect their young and have been known to injure people who come too close.

The **yellow mongoose** is a common grassland carnivore that feeds mainly on insects but also small mammals, birds and even snakes. Some have also learned to survive in cities by scavenging in human refuse. They can't eat **wandering donkey acraea** butterflies though, because their caterpillars eat poisonous plants, making the butterflies poisonous too!

Yellow Mongoose

Blue Cranes

The **mountain zebra** is a rare type of zebra found in Highveld grassland and mountainous areas of South Africa. It was almost hunted to extinction, but still survives in a few special nature reserves.

Similarly, the **black wildebeest** used to roam South Africa in huge herds but was almost wiped out by European settlers and is now a rare, protected species.

HOW DO THEY LIVE THERE?

Wandering Donkey Acraea

Black Wildebeest

Mountain Zebra

Ground Squirrels

There are very few trees in the Highveld, so **Cape ground squirrels** live underground. Large groups live together in complicated systems of burrows which are often shared with mongooses and meerkats and can have up to 100 separate entrances.

One squirrel is always watching out for danger, and in hot weather they sometimes hold their big, bushy tail up as a sunshade to protect them from the hot sun!

Visit the Interactive Zone to see how ground squirrels behave, or try the **Interactive Map** on page 10 to see where the Highveld is located.

INTERACTIVE ZONE!

Scan the QR code to watch ground squirrels in the grasslands

(If you're not sure how, check page 6 for details.)

Cape Ground Squirrel

Fynbos

Along the southern coast is a special heathland habitat called fynbos, which has a huge variety of plant life and is only found in South Africa.

Ostriches are the world's biggest birds and also the fastest, running up to 70km per hour! They feed on seeds, fruit, insects and small animals in the fynbos.

One insect they never touch though is the brightly coloured **koppie foam grasshopper**, which eats poisonous milkweed then squirts the poison out as a thick, toxic foam when threatened!

Ostrich

Koppie Foam Grasshopper

WHAT LIVES IN THE FYNBOS?

Because fynbos is unique to South Africa, many of the plants and animals are endemic, which means they're found nowhere else in the world.

An example is the pretty little **pan opal butterfly.** The caterpillars produce drops of nectar to attract ants, and in return the ants protect them from predators like wasps and spiders.

Bontebok are antelopes that were nearly hunted to extinction, but conservationists saved them and now there are lots living in protected fynbos reserves.

Pan Opal Butterfly

Bontebok

Fynbos naturally burns in hot, dry weather and some of the plants can only flower and produce seeds after burning.

The **Cape sugarbird** is an endemic fynbos bird that is specially adapted to feed on the protea flowers that grow in burned areas.

Cape lappet moth caterpillars eat fynbos plants, but also many others and are found throughout southern Africa. The adult moths don't have a mouth and can't feed, so they have to rely on fat stored from when they were caterpillars.

HOW DO THEY LIVE THERE?

Cape Lappet Moth Caterpillar

Cape Sugarbird

INTERACTIVE ZONE!

Scan the QR code to see some different fynbos reptiles

(If you're not sure how, check page 6 for details.)

Fynbos Reptiles

Lots of different reptiles live in the fynbos, hiding safe underground during the regular natural fires.

One of the biggest is the **puff adder**, which is Africa's most dangerous snake... although like most snakes, they prefer to avoid people when they can.

Visit the Interactive Zone to see more puff adders and other fynbos reptiles, or try the **Interactive Map** on page 10 to see where the fynbos is located.

Puff Adder

Karoo

Much of the west and centre of the country is dry, stony desert called Karoo, which gets very hot in the day but very cold at night. Animals that live there have to be specially adapted to survive the harsh conditions.

Namaqua doves are small pigeons with very long tails found in dry, arid areas. **Rock monitors** are very large lizards that live in the karoo and eat almost any type of animal, including small tortoises, which they swallow whole!

Namaqua Dove

Rock Monitor Lizard

WHAT LIVES IN THE SUCCULENT KAROO?

Monkey Beetle

Namaqua Sandgrouse

There are two types of Karoo. Succulent Karoo in the west gets its name from the succulent plants that grow there. They cope with dry conditions by storing water in their fleshy leaves.

Cape hares get water by eating the fleshy succulent leaves, but Namaqua sandgrouse sometimes have to fly as far as 60 kilometres to find it. The feathers on their belly are adapted to soak the water up so they can carry it back to the chicks in their nest!

The **monkey beetle** on the left looks as if it has crash-landed in the middle of a flower... but it's actually feeding on the pollen.

Succulent Flower

Cape Hare

WHAT LIVES IN THE NAMA KAROO?

Karoo Prinia

Towards the centre of the country is the dry, stony Nama Karoo. It's home to the noisy little **Karoo prinia,** which feeds on small invertebrates, and the **lobed argiope spider**, which is disguised as a spiny dead plant so the prinia won't spot it.

Attractive **gemsbok** are large antelopes that can go a long time without water. They use their long, straight horns to defend themselves and, like the African buffalo, have occasionally been known to kill lions that attack them.

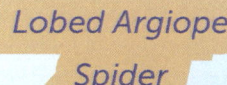
Lobed Argiope Spider

Gemsbok (South African Oryx)

INTERACTIVE ZONE!

Scan the QR code to watch a sand wasp digging her burrow

(If you're not sure how, check page 6 for details.)

Sand Wasps

Sand wasps dig burrows in dry ground, using their powerful jaws to carry the sand away. Then they catch a large caterpillar, which is sometimes so big they have to drag it back to the burrow along the ground!

They lay a single egg on the caterpillar then seal the burrow entrance. Inside, the wasp grub feeds on the caterpillar until it's an adult and can dig its way out.

Visit the Interactive Zone to watch a sand wasp digging its burrow, or try the **Interactive Map** on page 10 to see where succulent and Nama Karoo are located.

Sand Wasp

The Coast

South Africa has a huge coastline, running for nearly 3,000 kilometres, which makes it one of the best places in the world to see whales and dolphins. The massive **southern right whale** is one of about 40 different species, and can be recognised by its unusual double spout.

Many types of seabird can also be seen off the coast, including the **shy albatross,** which roams right across the world's southern oceans and has been recorded flying 1,000 kilometres in one day!

Shy Albatross

Southern Right Whale

WHAT LIVES ON THE COAST?

The tide that comes in twice a day brings with it a fresh supply of marine animals and plants, which provide food for all sorts of different seashore life.

Sea anemones look like pretty flowers but are actually little predators! They use poisonous stings in their tentacles to catch and eat animals like shrimps and fish. **Mussels** are shellfish that live in big colonies called 'mussel beds' and feed on tiny plankton in the sea water.

Grey Heron

False Plum Anemone

Many different birds also live on the seashore. **African oystercatchers** like to eat the mussels, using their strong, red beaks to prise open their protective shells. **Grey herons** patrol the seashore in search of fish, crabs and even small birds and mammals, which they catch with a lightning strike from their long yellow beak.

Endangered **Cape cormorants** are only found on the coast of southern Africa, where they nest in big colonies on rocky cliffs and seashore. They are superb swimmers, catching fish by chasing them underwater.

HOW DO THEY SURVIVE THERE?

Cape Cormorant

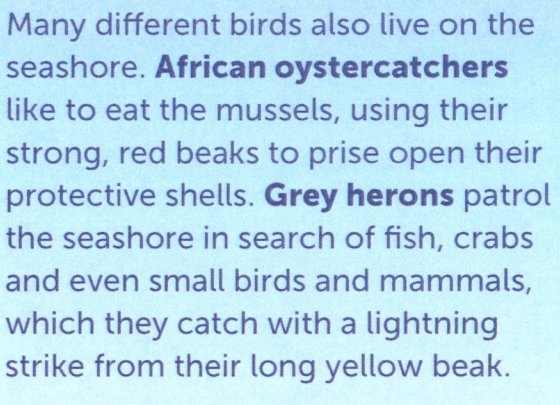
Mussels

African Oystercatcher

INTERACTIVE ZONE!

Scan the QR code to see fur seals on the coast

(If you're not sure how, check page 6 for details.)

Fur Seals

Fur seals are large carnivores that spend most of their lives at sea feeding on fish and other marine animals, such as squid and crabs. They can dive to a depth of over 200 metres and hold their breath for up to 7 minutes!

Cape fur seals breed in large, noisy colonies around the coasts of southern Africa. They used to be hunted for their thick fur but are protected now.

Visit the Interactive Zone to see more Cape fur seals.

Cape Fur Seals

Iconic South African Animals

South Africa has a huge variety of different animals, which makes it very difficult to pick out the most iconic... but I've chosen five groups which I think stand out.

- **African Penguins**
- **Herbivores**
- **Baboons**
- **Carnivores**
- **Meerkats**

African Penguins

Penguins are some of the world's favourite birds, famous for their cute, waddling walk. They are popular children's toys and have starred in many TV shows and films.

Although they can't fly and are clumsy on land, penguins are superb swimmers, using their flipper-like wings to 'fly' through the water after fish, which are their favourite food.

African penguins breed around the coast of southern Africa. There used to be so many that their poo (called guano) built up in huge piles and they burrowed inside to make their nests! But people collected the guano for fertiliser, so now they nest in the open.

Sadly, their numbers have fallen dramatically over the last 60 years, due firstly to egg-collecting and pollution, and more recently lack of food because of over-fishing by people. Now they are an endangered species, and conservationists are fighting to save them from extinction.

African penguins used to be called 'jackass penguins' because of their loud call that sounds like a donkey braying. Visit the **Interactive Zone** to see more African penguins and listen to them calling.

INTERACTIVE ZONE!

Scan the QR code to see and hear more African penguins

(If you're not sure how, check page 6 for details.)

Herbivores

Herbivores are animals that eat plants, and South Africa has a huge range of different types, from enormous elephants to tiny mice (not to mention all the insects and birds!).

Springboks are the national animal of South Africa. The name means 'jumping antelope' and comes from a strange display called 'pronking', where males leap into the air with their backs arched.

Springbok Pronking

Secretive little **klipspringers** live in pairs on steep, rocky cliffs, mainly feeding at night. The **greater kudu** with its impressive spiral horns is one of Africa's biggest antelopes, and males wander savanna and thickets alone during the daytime.

Visit the **Interactive Zone** to learn more about South Africa's many different herbivorous mammals.

Klipspringer

Greater Kudu

INTERACTIVE ZONE!

Scan the QR code to watch more South African herbivores

(If you're not sure how, check page 6 for details.)

Chacma Baboons

Chacma baboons are large monkeys that live in troops of up to a hundred throughout South Africa, in all habitats except desert.

Their diet includes almost every sort of food, from plants, fruit and seeds to insects, reptiles, birds and small mammals.

Feeding

Adult Male

They also raid human rubbish in towns and cities and even break into houses and cars in search of food. Because of this they are sometimes treated as pests and signs are put up warning people not to feed them.

Grooming each other is an important bonding activity for the members of a troop, and also helps keep them healthy.

Predators like lions, leopards and eagles hunt them, but males fight very aggressively to defend the troop, and can cause serious injuries with their powerful jaws.

Visit the **Interactive Zone** to watch some of South Africa's chacma baboons.

BABOONS are dangerous WILD animals
- DO NOT FEED -
Keep Doors Locked and Windows Closed

Mother and Baby

INTERACTIVE ZONE!

Scan the QR code to see more chacma baboons

(If you're not sure how, check page 6 for details.)

Grooming

Carnivores

The word 'carnivore' means 'meat eater'. It's sometimes used to refer to fish, reptiles and even insect-eating plants! But I'm concentrating on mammals that eat other mammals... and South Africa is one of the best places in the world to see them.

They include cats, dogs, hyenas, civets and mongooses, and range in size from huge lions patrolling the savanna to tiny dwarf mongooses catching mice in the grasslands.

Spotted Hyena

Male Lion

Lions are extremely powerful predators that hunt large herbivores like zebra and wildebeest. Over half their body is muscle... the most of any mammal.

Spotted hyenas are the most common African carnivore, living in large social groups led by a dominant female. They have a reputation as cowardly, stupid scavengers, but are actually highly intelligent and skilful hunters.

Black-backed jackals, on the other hand, often scavenge dead meat, as well as eating lizards, snakes, insects and sometimes fruit and berries.

Visit the **Interactive Zone** to see more of South Africa's carnivores.

INTERACTIVE ZONE!

Scan the QR code to see more South African carnivores

(If you're not sure how, check page 6 for details.)

Black-backed Jackal

Meerkats

Meerkats are another animal that's famous around the world from films and TV, and also popular as a children's toy... but the truth is very different from their cute, cuddly image!

They are actually members of the mongoose family, and fierce predators. Their main food is insects, spiders and scorpions but they also catch and eat amphibians, small mammals, birds, lizards and even snakes!

Meerkats live in large social groups of up to 40 called 'mobs'. Their home is a complex burrow system as big as five metres across, with many different entrances and exits. They use it to raise their young, shelter from extreme weather and stay safe from predators.

Guard Duty

Meerkat mobs are led by a dominant male and female who are the only ones that have babies. All the other adults take turns collecting food, caring for the dominant pair's babies and looking out for danger.

Lookouts pick a high point, like a termite mound, and stand on their hind legs scanning for danger. If they spot a predator such as an eagle, they give a series of high-pitched squeals to warn the rest of the group, who dive into a burrow for safety.

Visit the **Interactive Zone** to watch a colony of South African meerkats and see how they behave.

Threatening

Play-fighting

INTERACTIVE ZONE!

Scan the QR code to see some meerkats in action!

(If you're not sure how, check page 6 for details.)

Conserving South Africa's Wildlife

WHAT ARE THE PROBLEMS?

Crops need to be watered due to lack of rain

As in most countries around the world, South Africa's wildlife faces challenges.

Illegal poaching has long been a problem, with hundreds of rhinos killed each year for their horns, which are used in Chinese medicine. Animals like elephants, pangolin and various reptiles are also taken.

South Africa is a very dry country, and climate change is making this worse, with droughts becoming more common. Pollution from the country's huge coal power stations is adding to the problem.

As a result, some animals are struggling to survive in their traditional habitat.

Female Kudu looking for water in a dried up riverbed

Rhino horns in a Chinese shop

HOW CAN THEY BE FIXED?

Marine Protected Area around the Cape Nature Reserve

Increasing sea temperatures together with over-fishing and pollution such as plastics are affecting sea life, with the numbers of sharks, penguins and fish all falling.

The good news is that there are many people in South Africa working really hard to try and solve these problems.

Dedicated teams are fighting to catch the poachers, wind and solar farms are being built to produce renewable energy, and Marine Protected Areas have been set up to preserve the oceans.

Hopefully, these measures can protect South Africa's amazing variety of wildlife for future generations to enjoy!

Young fur seal with plastic wrapped around its chest

The number of sharks seen has fallen

Index

Aardvark 14
Acraea Butterfly 20–21
African Buffalo 17
African Common White 13
African Elephant 15, 18
African Oystercatcher 33
African Penguin 35, 36–37
Beetles 16, 18, 28, 50
Black-backed Jackal 35, 43
Black Girdled Lizard 25, 50
Black Rhinoceros 17
Black Wildebeest 20–21
Blue Crane 20, 50
Bontebok 24
Butterflies 13, 20–21, 24
Cape Cormorant 32–33, 50
Cape Fur Seal 34, 47
Cape Grassbird 19
Cape Ground Squirrel 22
Cape Gull 33, 50
Cape Hare 28

Cape Sugarbird 25
Carnivores 42–43
Chacma Baboon 35
Cheetah 11
Common Duiker 1
Conservation 46–47
Double-collared Sunbird 16
Dung Beetle 16, 18, 50
False Plum Anemone 32
Fynbos 23–26
Gemsbok 29
Giraffe 12–13, 50
Grass Mouse 19
Greater Kudu 39, 46
Grey Heron 32
Helmeted Guineafowl 20, 50
Herbivores 38–39
Highveld Grassland 19–22
Jackal Buzzard 24, 50
Karoo 27–30
Karoo Prinia 29

Klipspringer 39
Koppie Foam Grasshopper 23, 43, 50
Kori Bustard 12
Lappet Moth Caterpillar 25
Leopard Tortoise 16
Lion 42–43
Little Swift 29, 50
Lizards 25, 27, 50
Lobed Argiope Spider 29
Locust 39, 50
Map of South Africa 8, 10
Marine Protected Area 47
Martial Eagle 11
Meerkat 35, 44–45
Millipede Assassin Bug 45, 50
Monkey Beetle 28
Mountain Zebra 21
Mussels 33
Namaqua Dove 27
Namaqua Sandgrouse 28
Ostrich 12, 23, 50
Pan Opal Butterfly 24
Poaching 17, 46
Praying Mantis 28, 50

Puff Adder 26
QR Codes 6, 10, 14, 18, 22, 26, 30, 34, 37, 39, 41, 43, 45, 50
Red Bishop 54
Red-faced Mousebird 15
Rhino 17, 46
Rock Monitor Lizard 27
Sacred Ibis 9, 50
Sand Wasp 30
Savanna 11–14
Sharks 47
Shy Albatross 31
South African Oryx 29
Southern Right Whale 31
Spotted Hyena 42–43
Springbok 35, 38
Spring Hare 38, 50
Succulent 28
Swift Tern 9, 50
The Coast 31–34
Thickets & Woodland 15–18
White-backed Vulture 13, 50
Yellow-billed Hornbill 12
Yellow Mongoose 20

Wildlife Extras!

On some pages, there are photos of animals that haven't been labelled, usually in the background or hidden in vegetation.

See how many you can spot, then check the list below to see if you got them all. You can also scan the QR code above to find out more about them.

Page	Animals
9	Two sacred ibis on the shore and three swift terns flying over the beach.
12	An ostrich in the left-hand corner and three giraffes to the right.
13	Two white-backed vultures flying behind the giraffes.
16	A giant dung beetle in front of the tortoise.
20	Two blue cranes flying behind the mongoose, and four helmeted guineafowl feeding in the grass on the right.
24	A jackal buzzard flying on the left behind the bontebok.
25	A black girdled lizard sitting on a rock on the right.
28	A praying mantis nymph on the succulent to the right.
29	Three little swifts flying behind the horns of the gemsbok.
32,33	Five Cape cormorants flying across the centre and three Cape gulls on the right-hand side, one flying and two perched on the shore.
38	A spring hare in the grass on the right-hand side at the front.
39	A desert locust on the bush in front of the kudu.
43	A koppie foam grasshopper on the ground in front of the jackal.
45	A millipede assassin bug by the stone in front of the fighting meerkats.

Acknowledgements

Many people helped me with my photography in South Africa and with the writing of this book. I would like to thank some of them here:

Dominic Chadbon (The Fynbos Guy) for guiding me around the Western Cape and introducing me to the amazing wildlife of the region.

The many wonderful staff at the National Parks I visited, for their hard work, patience and advice on how to find wildlife.

Celeste and Nicole of the Cheriton Guest House, for their advice and support when staying at the Cape.

Endrik, Andre and Johan of de Hoop Collection who rescued me when I broke down in the remote veld.

Ellie Owen at Rowanvale for her astute, invaluable editorial advice.

All photos, video clips and sound recordings of wildlife in this book and on the associated web pages were taken by Hugh Lansdown in South Africa except; the rhino horns photo on page 46 which was taken in China, and both the elephant shrew video in 'elephant relatives' and the white-backed vultures photo in 'Wildlife Extras', which were taken across the border in Namibia.

All animals were wild and free, and living in their natural habitat.

About the Author

Hugh Lansdown is a Welsh wildlife photographer who has travelled extensively, and his images have appeared in hundreds of books, magazines and other publications across the globe.

He is also heavily involved in conservation at home in Wales, working for local wildlife charities, carrying out habitat management work and giving talks about wildlife conservation.

You can find out more about Hugh's photography, writing and conservation work by visiting his website or signing up to his monthly newsletters:

www.hughlansdown.com/newsletters.html

Sneaky Animals!

A few random animals seem to have sneaked into the book when Hugh wasn't looking...

Page 2 - a vlei rat

Page 3 - three great white pelicans (though they're actually pink!)

Page 5 - a greater flamingo and two hartebeest

Page 6 - a Bowker's sapphire butterfly and a black savanna wasp

Page 7 - a booted eagle

Page 48 - a branched ermine moth

Page 53 - a golden-breasted bunting

What did you think of Wildlife of the World - South Africa?

A big thank you for buying this book. It means a lot that you chose this book specifically from such a wide range on offer.

We do hope you enjoyed it.

Book reviews are incredibly important for an author. All feedback helps them improve their writing for future projects and for developing this edition. If you are able to spare a few minutes to post a review on Amazon or Goodreads, that would be much appreciated.

Southern Red Bishop in Karoo National Park

www.ingramcontent.com/pod-product-compliance
Lightning Source LLC
Chambersburg PA
CBRC100222100526
44590CB00008B/147